THE OLYMPICS

ANCIENT OLYMPICS

JACKIE GAFF

Heinemann Library
Chicago, Illinois

Customer Service 888-454-2279
Visit our website at www.heinemannlibrary.com

Designed by Ticktock Media and Tim Bones
Originated by Ambassador Litho Ltd.
Printed and Bound in China by South China Printing Company

08 07 06 05 04
10 9 8 7 6 5 4 3 2 1

Library of Congress Cataloging-in-Publication Data
Gaff, Jackie.
Ancient Olympics / Jackie Gaff.
       p. cm. -- (Olympics)
Summary: Provides an overview of how the Olympics began in ancient Greece and a look at each day's festivities.
Includes bibliographical references and index.
ISBN 1-4034-4676-8 (Library Binding-hardcover)
1. Olympic games (Ancient)--Juvenile literature. [1. Olympic games (Ancient)] I. Title. II. Olympics (2003)
GV23.G34 2003
796.48--dc21

                                   2003006936

Acknowledgments
The author and publisher are grateful to the following for permission to reproduce copyright material:
pp. 4t, 9t, 11t, 13b, 18b, 18–19t, 20l, 20c, 24l, 27t, 29b Corbis; 6t Alamy; 6b, 7b, 8b, 11b, 12t, 23b, 25t, 26t, 26b Ancient Art & Architecture; 16c Heritage Images; 28t, 28b Empics. Cover photographs: main photo by Alamy; other photos by Corbis.

Every effort has been made to contact copyright holders of any material reproduced in this book. Any omissions will be rectified in subsequent printings if notice is given to the publisher.

For more information on the statue of a discus thrower that appears on the cover of this book, turn to page 20. The main cover image shows the palaestra, a place in ancient Greece where athletes learned how to wrestle. The center image shows a sculpture from about 350 B.C.E. in which runners are approaching a Greek goddess. The other cover image shows two wrestlers painted by a Greek artist in about 530 B.C.E. For more information on the images that appear on the back cover of this book, turn to page 17.

CONTENTS

Some words are shown in bold, **like this.** You can find out what they mean by looking in the glossary.

The Land and People of Ancient Greece

The Parthenon, shown above, was built in Athens between 447–432 B.C.E.

In ancient times, the Olympic Games were held in a place called Olympia, in southwestern Greece. Ancient Greece was not a single nation as Greece is today. Instead, by the 770s B.C.E., Greece was made up of a number of independent **city-states** called **poleis.** The city-states were located throughout Greece and the islands of the Aegean and Ionian seas. They were also located along the coast of what is today the country of Turkey.

Some Greeks were also starting to settle elsewhere. By the 500s B.C.E., Greeks had founded **colonies** near the Black Sea and the Mediterranean Sea. Greece is a mountainous country, with thin, rocky soil and little good land. Farmers had to work hard to produce food to eat. The city-states were in the most **fertile** areas, which were the coastal and inland plains and the valleys between the mountains.

LIFE IN ANCIENT GREECE
FARMERS

In some ways, life in ancient Greece was similar to life today. For example, foods raised by farmers in ancient Greece were similar to foods of today. Ancient Greek farmers herded goats and sheep for their milk, meat, and wool. They raised pigs and chickens and kept bees to make honey. The most important crops were grains that were ground into flour, grapes used to make wine, and olives, which were crushed for their oil. People used olive oil to make soap, for cooking, and as a fuel for lamps. In the most fertile areas, farmers grew fruit, nuts, and vegetables such as peas, beans, carrots, and lettuce.

Before the first Olympics were held, each city-state was ruled by a king or another powerful person. By the time the Olympics first began, however, some city-states had adopted a system in which all **citizens** shared in running the government. This system is called **democracy.** It was first put into practice in the city-state of Athens in about 500 B.C.E.

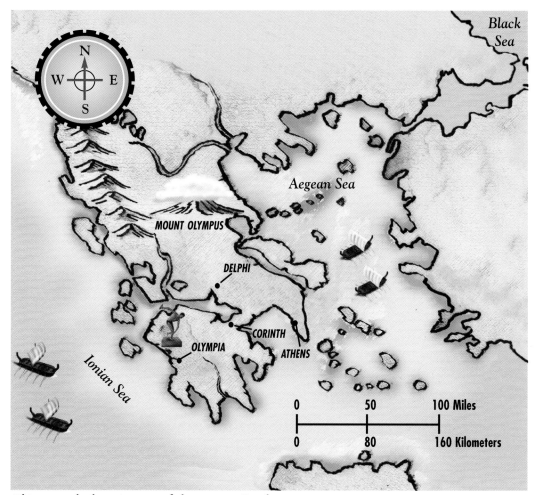

This artwork shows a map of the ancient Greek empire.

OLYMPIC YEARS

The first Olympic Games took place in about 776 B.C.E. The abbreviation B.C.E. after a date means "before the common era." This is used instead of the old abbreviation, B.C. The years are counted backward toward zero. The abbreviation C.E is used for years after zero. It stands for "common era."

ANCIENT GREEK SOCIETY

In the democratic city-states of ancient Greece, only men who owned property or land were allowed to take part in the running of the government.

*Women were not considered to be **citizens,** and they had no political rights. Ancient Greeks believed women were the responsibility of their male relatives.*

*Other people in Greek society were **slaves.** Most slaves were people from other countries who were captured during a war or by pirates. Slaves and their children were thought of as their owner's property. Like women, they had no rights.*

Zeus's Sanctuary at Olympia

Long before the Olympic Games were first held in Olympia, the **city-states** had been important as **sanctuaries,** or holy places. For centuries, Greek people had traveled there to worship Zeus, the king of their gods. The ancient Greek people named Olympia in honor of the place where they believed Zeus lived, Mount Olympus. At 9,570 feet (2,917 meters) high, this mountain is the highest peak in Greece.

This photo shows what Mount Olympus looks like today.

LIFE IN ANCIENT GREECE
PRIESTS AND PRIESTESSES

People believed in many gods and goddesses in ancient Greece. Female priests, or priestesses, served the goddesses, while male priests served the gods. Most priests and priestesses worked full-time, but some priests and priestesses were ordinary **citizens** who served for two to four years, or just during religious festivals. Their duties ranged from supervising **rituals** to conducting weddings and funerals. Priests and priestesses were not paid money. Instead they were given free meals and a place to live.

This head of a bronze statue of the god Zeus was made during the 400s B.C.E.

OLYMPIAN GODS

Ancient Greek people believed that Zeus shared his home on Mount Olympus with his wife, Hera, and a family of ten other gods and goddesses.

Zeus—king of the gods and god of justice, law, thunder, lightning, and rain

Hera—Zeus's wife and goddess of women, marriage, and mothers

*Aphrodite—goddess of love, beauty, and **fertility***

Apollo—god of music, light, healing, archery, and farming

Ares—god of war

Artemis—goddess of hunting, wildlife, purity, and childbirth

Athena—goddess of cities, war, and wisdom

Demeter—goddess of grain crops and farming

Dionysus—god of grapes, wine, and pleasure

Hephaestus—god of fire and crafts

Hermes—messenger of the gods and the god of fertility, fortune, and roads

Poseidon—god of the sea, water, horses, and earthquakes

AMAZING FACT

According to a Greek myth, the Olympic Games were founded by Zeus. The story tells how Zeus wrestled with his father, Kronos, at Olympia to win control of the world. To celebrate his victory, Zeus held a series of contests for the gods.

The ancient Greeks believed their gods had the power to harm or help the lives of ordinary humans. They thought the best way to please the gods was to make a **sacrifice** to them. A sacrifice may have been made by pouring wine at a place of worship or by killing an animal there. At first there were no temples or other buildings at Olympia. It was simply a clearing within a sacred grove of trees, known as the **Altis.** Structures were built there beginning in the 500s B.C.E. In the 400s B.C.E., a magnificent temple was built to honor Zeus.

This model shows what Olympia might have looked like.

Games in the Greek World

Exercise was very important to the people of ancient Greece. The **city-states** were often at war with one another, and exercise was a way for soldiers to stay in shape. Athletic contests were also a way to worship the gods. Athletes paid tribute to the gods by showing how strong or fast they were.

An athletic contest was a part of many local religious festivals, but there were also four major festivals that drew athletes from all over Greece. These festivals were called the Panhellenic games. *Pan* is a word that means "all," and *hellenic* means "Greek." The games included the Olympic, Pythian, Isthmian, and Nemean festivals. One of these festivals was held every year, with each festival repeated once every four years in turn. This period of four years was known as an Olympiad. Together, the competitions were known as the *periodos*. An athlete who won at all four festivals was called a *periodonikes*.

This is a bronze statue of a female runner made around 530 B.C.E. Women were not allowed to take part in the Olympics, but they held their own races at Olympia every four years.

PANHELLENIC GAMES

OLYMPIC GAMES
the first national Games, held in honor of Zeus, the king of the gods

PYTHIAN GAMES
celebrated at Delphi, in honor of Apollo

ISTHMIAN GAMES
held at Corinth, in honor of Poseidon

NEMEAN GAMES
*held in honor of Zeus at his **sanctuary** in Nemea, near Corinth*

OLYMPIC HEROES

The wrestler Milon of Croton was a sports superhero. He won the boys' wrestling contest in 540 B.C.E. Later, he won the men's wrestling contest at five Olympic Games in a row. He also won 25 contests at the other Panhellenic games. He was a periodonikes an amazing five times!

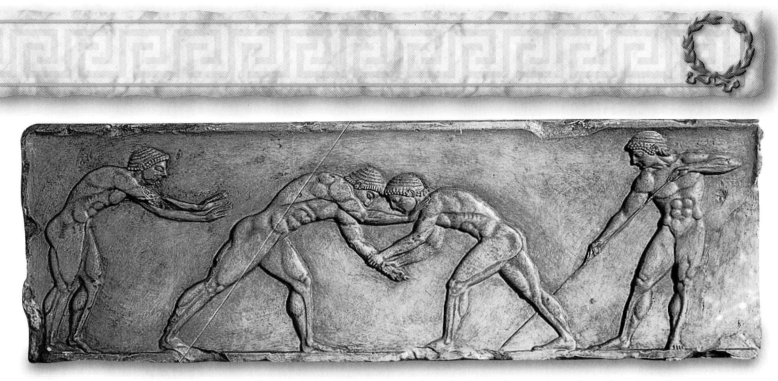

This wrestling scene was carved on the base of a statue made in the 400s B.C.E. Wrestling contests took place on the first day of the games.

No one knows exactly when the first Olympic Games were held, but the Greeks first recorded the date of these games in 776 B.C.E. By 572 B.C.E., the event had become the most important of the Panhellenic festivals.

This Greek vase was made in the 500s B.C.E. It shows Olympic athletes running and jumping.

LIFE IN ANCIENT GREECE
PAIDOTRIBES (SPORTS TEACHERS)

Only boys went to school in ancient Greece. They started at the age of seven, and sports was an important part of their education, along with reading, writing, and music.

Sports teachers were called *paidotribes*. They taught everything from running to wrestling. A number of athletes in the ancient Olympics were trained in their boyhood by *paidotribes*.

Rules of the Games

The Olympic Games were held every four years, in August or September. At first, only one race—the sprint—was held, and the games only lasted one day. Gradually, more events were added, and by the end of the 400s B.C.E., the games lasted for five days.

By about 400 B.C.E., the Olympic Games were organized and controlled by Elis, a **city-state** near Olympia. In the spring of an Olympic year, three **heralds** from Elis visited every part of Greece to announce an Olympic truce to stop any wars. At this time, many wars were fought in Greece. The truce was an agreement that no wars were allowed for a period of up to three months. Athletes and **spectators** could travel to and from Olympia in safety. Any **poleis** that failed to observe the truce were fined heavily.

AMAZING FACT

In 404 B.C.E., a mother disguised herself as her son's trainer so she could watch him compete in the games. Her son won, but her disguise was discovered. She was not punished, but a new Olympic rule was introduced. It said that the athletes' trainers had to be completely unclothed when they registered for the Olympic Games!

These are ruins of the temple of Hera at Olympia. The terms of a truce called during each Olympic Games were engraved on a discus and kept at this temple.

Only Greek **citizens** were allowed to compete in the games, which meant the competition was open to males only. Women and **slaves** were not allowed to take part. Married women were not allowed to watch or visit the games. Only single women could. Women who disobeyed this rule were severely punished. According to the writer Pausanias, who lived in the 100s B.C.E., any married woman found at Olympia during the games was thrown to her death from a nearby cliff.

This statue of Hermes, messenger of the gods, dates from the 300s B.C.E. Ancient Greeks believed that Hermes protected heralds.

LIFE IN ANCIENT GREECE
HERALDS

Heralds were government officials who traveled throughout Greece carrying important messages for poleis. They held a special stick as a sign of their authority. It was believed that they were protected by the messenger god Hermes.

People were not allowed to attack them, not even during wars. In addition to announcing the truce and the dates of the Olympic Games, heralds also acted as legal advisers to citizens of their poleis.

The only married woman allowed to attend the ancient Olympics was the priestess of the goddess Demeter. A statue of Demeter is shown above.

Pregame Training

On the first day of the five-day ancient Olympic Games, the athletes, their trainers, and the judges all gathered together inside the **Altis.** This large, enclosed area was the most sacred part of Olympia. The ancient Greeks believed that the god Zeus had lived in this holy place. During a ceremony in the Altis, priests checked that each athlete was allowed to take part in the festival. If the priests found out that an athlete was not Greek or was a **slave,** the athlete was asked to leave immediately.

This Greek vase dating from the 300s B.C.E. shows two competing boxers.

AMAZING FACT

In 93 C.E., a boxer named Apollonius arrived late to Elis, claiming that bad weather had delayed his ship. In fact, he had been winning cash prizes at other games. This was discovered, and he was disqualified by the hellanodikes, or judge, who named Apollonius's opponent the winner.

LIFE IN ANCIENT GREECE
GYMNOTRIBAI (PERSONAL TRAINERS)

Gymnotribai were experts and trainers in particular sports. Sometimes they were former Olympic champions. Ikkos of Tarentum, for example, wrote a book on athletic training and is thought to have won the pentathlon in 444 B.C.E. The pentathlon is a competition that includes five different events.

While an athlete practiced, the *gymnotribai* would watch the athlete closely and suggest ways to improve the athlete's technique. Afterward, the *gymnotribai* might give the athlete a massage. Some *gymnotribai* were also healers who could help with sports injuries.

Athletes were supposed to have been in training for ten months before their arrival in Elis. Once in the city, they had to follow a strict diet and a hard exercise program set by the **hellanodikai.** Many athletes were in Elis with their own private trainers, who advised them on training and diet, too. Athletes were supposed to stay away from fattening desserts and to eat high-protein foods such as meat and fish to build up their strength.

An athlete's diet usually included octopus and squid, which were boiled or fried in olive oil. The octopuses shown here have been hung out to dry in the sun.

This is a shallow Greek drinking cup called a kylix made in 470 B.C.E. It shows a Greek athlete cleaning up after a competition. Before contests, contestants would rub olive oil over their bodies. This helped prevent minor skin injuries and keep pores free from dirt. After an event had finished, dirty athletes used a scraper called a strigil to remove the oil and dirt from their bodies.

TRAINING PLACES

All Greek cities had special exercise centers. There were two main types: a gymnasium was a large public place open to all **citizens,** while a **palaestra** was smaller and was not open to everyone. Both were built around an open exercise courtyard that was surrounded by covered rows of columns, which provided shelter during bad weather. There were also changing rooms, bathrooms, and meeting rooms.

At Olympia, the palaestra was actually attached to the gymnasium, and both places were probably only used by competing athletes and their trainers.

A Tour of Olympia

By the 100s B.C.E., people had built many magnificent stone temples and sports facilities in Olympia. The **Altis** remained at Olympia's center and by this time was enclosed by walls and **colonnades.** Inside the Altis were three temples—one dedicated to Zeus and the others to his wife, Hera, and his mother, Rhea. There were also many outdoor **altars** and statues of the gods.

One of these altars was called the Pelopion. It was the **sanctuary** of a local hero named Pelops, who competed in one of the first chariot races held at the Olympic Games. Another altar was known as the Philippeion. It was built in the 300s B.C.E. to celebrate King Philip II of Macedon's military victories and triumphs in Olympic chariot races. King Philip's son, Alexander the Great, completed the building of the Philippeion altar and even competed in the games himself.

AMAZING FACT

The Olympic hero Pelops was said to have won a chariot race against Oinomaos, who was king of a city near Olympia. One Greek *legend* tells how Pelops was helped by the god Poseidon, who gave him a golden chariot pulled by four winged horses.

These are the ruins of the gate to the Olympia stadium. The stadium was built between 775 to 350 B.C.E. It was built to hold about 40,000 people.

This photo shows the colonnades in the Olympia stadium. Ancient Greeks believed that the stadium's dimensions were drawn up by the god Hercules.

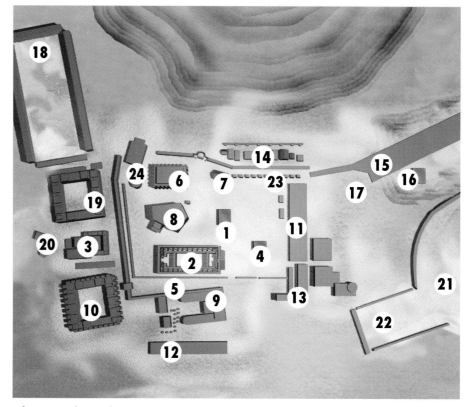
This map shows the main sites in Olympia.

To the northeast of the Altis were the athletes' gymnasium and **palaestra,** with an underground bathhouse and swimming pool. Running races were held in the stadium to the east of the Altis, and horse races took place in the **hippodrome.** The Bouleuterion was a house where Olympic organizers met. To the west was the Leonidaion, a luxury hotel for visiting officials and other important people. Other buildings called treasuries were located north of the Altis. Precious items that would be offered to the god Zeus were kept there.

MAP KEY

1. Great Altar of Zeus
2. Temple of Zeus
3. Workshop of the sculptor Phidias, who carved the 43-foot- (13-meter-) high statue of Zeus in the temple
4. Statue of the winged goddess of victory
5. Sacred olive tree—winners' wreaths were woven from its leaves and branches
6. Altar and temple of Hera
7. Altar and temple of Rhea
8. Pelopion
9. Bouleuterion
10. Leonidaion
11. Echo colonnade
12. Southern colonnade
13. Southeastern colonnade
14. Treasuries
15. Stadium
16. Judges' stand
17. Stadium entrance tunnel
18. Gymnasium
19. Palaestra
20. Bathhouses
21. Hippodrome
22. Starting gate
23. Zanes (statues of Zeus)
24. Philippeion

Gathering for the Games

Two days before the start of the five-day ancient Olympic festival, all the participants set out from Elis to walk in **procession** to Olympia. The **hellanodikai** led the way, followed by the athletes with their relatives and trainers, then the horses and the chariots. Their 36-mile (58-kilometer) route was called the Sacred Way. The journey included stops for religious **rituals,** such as the **sacrifice** of a pig, and overnight rest.

AMAZING FACT

Only a few hundred spectators traveled from nearby **poleis** in the early years of the Olympic Games. But by 100 C.E., they were coming from every corner of Greece and its **colonies,** and crowds had risen to more than 40,000 people!

Wealthy visitors or those coming from far away sailed up the Alpheios River to get to Olympia. Locals came on foot or by donkey. Some Greek people in rural communities still use donkeys for travel today.

This statue of a Greek actor was made in the 100s B.C.E. Actors and comedians were among the entertainers who amused ancient Olympic spectators.

Thousands of **spectators** were also arriving in Olympia from all around the Greek world. There were no restaurants at Olympia, and the only hotel was the Leonidaion. Wealthy visitors brought their own tents to sleep in, while less wealthy people used a blanket and slept on the ground. Traders put up stalls where they sold food and other goods, and craftspeople set up workshops where they made small statues for visitors to offer to the gods. Singers, musicians, poets, **conjurers,** and fortune-tellers provided entertainment. By the time the official procession arrived at Olympia, the site was like a huge bustling fairground humming with people and activity.

*These Greek coins were made in the **city-state** of Athens in about 480 B.C.E.*

LIFE IN ANCIENT GREECE

MARKET TRADERS

The thousands of spectators who arrived for the Olympic Games brought lots of business to market traders. In most Greek cities, markets were held in the agora—a large, open square surrounded by **colonnades.** The most successful traders had covered shops, but others had makeshift wooden stalls or simply laid their goods out in containers on the ground. Purchases were paid for with coins, but each poleis issued its own money, stamped with its unique symbol. In Athens, for example, coins featured the image of an owl, as seen in the image above.

Day One: The Games Begin!

The preparations were complete, and at long last the athletes could put their hard months of training to the test. The Olympics was above all a religious festival, however, and **rituals** were carried out daily. The opening ceremony took place in the Bouleuterion. At the ceremony, the athletes, their male relatives, and their trainers stood in front of a statue of Zeus and swore to obey the Olympic rules. The **hellanodikai** then swore that they would judge the competitors fairly. Afterwards, each athlete would visit one of the **altars** in the **Altis** to make an offering to their favorite god and pray for victory.

This photograph shows women dressed in clothing like women in ancient Greece wore. They are lighting a flame to mark the start of the 2000 Sydney Olympics.

DAY ONE PROGRAM OF EVENTS

MORNING
- *Swearing-in ceremony for competitors and judges*
- *Contests for heralds and trumpeters*
- *Running, boxing, and wrestling contests for boys*
- *Public and private prayers and **sacrifices***

AFTERNOON
- *Speeches and recitals by **philosophers,** historians, and poets*

This print from the 1800s shows an ancient Greek wrestling match. The two competitors are being watched by a hellanodikes.

The first contests were for trumpeters and **heralds.** The winners won the right to signal the start of other contests and to announce the results. The morning's events finished with running races for boys aged twelve to eighteen and with boxing and wrestling events. There were no events for the rest of the day, so first-time competitors could go sightseeing.

This painting of a Greek runner appears on a Greek vase made in the 500s B.C.E. Runners did not use a crouching start. They started from a standing position. The starting signal was either a trumpet blast or the shout "Apite!," which means "Go!"

LIFE IN ANCIENT GREECE

HELLANODIKAI (JUDGES)

As the games grew larger over the centuries, the number of *hellanodikai* grew from two to ten by 100 C.E. *Hellanodikai* were like a combination of modern-day Olympic organizers, judges, and umpires. They wore special purple robes to set them apart from ordinary **citizens,** who usually wore white. *Hellanodikai* awarded prizes to the winners and punished any competitor or trainer who broke the rules. Athletes who cheated were fined or, in the worst cases, whipped!

OLYMPIC HEROES

The most famous trumpeter of the ancient Olympics was Herodorus.

He won the trumpet contest in ten Olympic Games in a row between 328 and 292 B.C.E.

He was said to be so strong that he could blow two trumpets at once.

Day Two of the Games

The men's events began at sunrise on day two with the most spectacular and dangerous event of the games—the chariot races in the **hippodrome.** There were races for chariots pulled by four-horse teams and two-horse teams, over distances that ranged from about 2.5 miles (4 kilometers) to more than 8 miles (13 kilometers).

Each competitor drove a bouncing, swaying chariot, gripping the reins in one hand and urging on his horses with a whip held in the other hand. The greatest danger for a charioteer was smashing into an opponent's chariot and being thrown from his chariot and crushed underneath the horses.

This copy of a Greek statue made in the 400s B.C.E. shows a discus thrower. The discus was one of the five pentathlon events.

This painting on a Greek vase made in the 300s B.C.E. shows a chariot race. Chariot races were thought to be the most spectacular events of the games.

OLYMPIC HEROES

In the 400s B.C.E., Damonon of Sparta claimed he and his son had won 68 chariot races and horse races at 8 different festivals.

LIFE IN ANCIENT GREECE
CHARIOTEERS (CHARIOT DRIVERS)

Charioteers were famous for their skill and bravery. The sport was so dangerous that horse owners rarely drove their own teams, but used professional charioteers instead. It was also expensive—a racehorse could cost as much as three times the average annual salary! Although the job sounded glamorous, charioteers had all the hard work and little of the glory. If a team won a chariot race, the owner was awarded the Olympic crown and had his name recorded in the victory lists. All the charioteer received was a victory ribbon.

DAY TWO PROGRAM OF EVENTS

MORNING

- **Procession** of competitors into the hippodrome
  - Chariot races
  - Horse races

AFTERNOON

- The pentathlon—discus, javelin, long jump, running, and wrestling events

EVENING

- **Rituals** at the Pelopion in honor of the hero Pelops, including the **sacrifice** of a black ram
- Parade of winners around the **Altis** and the performance of specially written hymns sung in their honor
- Feasts and other celebrations

In the afternoon, the crowds gathered in the stadium for the pentathlon. Competitors began by hurling the discus—a flat, round disc weighing about 5.5 pounds (2.5 kilograms). Next, they threw a type of wooden spear called a javelin. This event was followed by the long jump. If one athlete had won all three events by this stage, he was declared the outright victor and the last two events—running and wrestling—were canceled.

This painting on a Greek vase made in the 400s B.C.E. shows a long jumper in action.

Day Three of the Games

This wall painting, created in the 500s B.C.E., shows an animal being prepared for sacrifice.

The third day of the Olympic Games was the religious high point of the entire Olympic festival. A great **sacrifice** of 100 oxen donated by the **citizens** of Elis was made to Zeus. The **ritual** began with a grand **procession** around the **Altis** by the ten **hellanodikai,** ambassadors from the Greek **city-states,** all the competitors and their trainers, and, finally, the **sacrificial** animals.

The sacrifice took place at the Great **Altar** of Zeus, which was outside Zeus's temple. After the animals were killed, their legs were burned on the altar. By the 100s C.E., a mound of ash 23 feet (7 meters) high had built up from the hundreds of sacrifices. The rest of the oxen's bodies were roasted and eaten at a public banquet in the evening.

DAY THREE PROGRAM OF EVENTS

MORNING

• Grand procession around the Altis by important people and competitors

• Sacrifice of 100 oxen at the Great Altar of Zeus

AFTERNOON

• Running races—the short stade, medium-distance diaulos, and long-distance dolichos

• Great banquet for everyone, from important people to **spectators**

OLYMPIC HEROES

The greatest and most famous ancient Olympic runner was Leonidas of Rhodes. He was said to move with the speed of a god, and he won all three running races at the four Olympic Games between 164 to 152 B.C.E.

The afternoon was taken up by races in the stadium. The shortest race, the **stade,** was a straight dash down one length of the stadium—about 630 feet (192 meters). The other two races were the **diaulos,** which was two stadium lengths, and the long-distance **dolichos,** which was 20–24 lengths. Some men competed in more than one event, and the rare athlete who won all three at the same Olympics was called a *triastes*.

These three figures appear on a Greek vase dating from the 400s B.C.E. They illustrate the fact that there were three different types of running races held on day three of the games.

LIFE IN ANCIENT GREECE

ATHLETES

Athletes came from all levels of Greek society. What mattered was the individual's skill and strength. Since there were no second or third prizes, most athletes wanted to win. There were no team events, and each athlete represented himself, not his home city.

The *stade* race was the earliest and only event at the first thirteen Olympic Games. Over the following centuries, winning this contest remained such an honor that the next Olympic Games held were always named after the winner of the *stade* race.

Day Four of the Games

This statue of a boxer was made between 1 B.C.E. and 100 B.C.E. Boxers at the ancient Olympics wore little protection, unlike fighters of today.

Much of the fourth day of the ancient Olympics was spent at the **palaestra.** This was the place for wrestling, boxing, and the **pancratium,** which was an event that combined boxing and wrestling. The fights were brutal, with few rules and no time limits—pairs of men fought until one of them won. The aim in wrestling was to get the opponent's shoulders, back, or hip on the ground. This was called a fall, and three falls meant the fight was over. Boxing matches could go on for hours, until one contestant gave up or was knocked out. Boxers did not wear padded gloves as boxers do today. Their hands were protected, but their fingers were left free. The only banned move was sticking the thumbs in the opponent's eyes!

OLYMPIC HEROES

In his 22-year career in the early 400s B.C.E., Theagenes of Thasos had 23 victories in boxing and the pancratium at the Olympics and other games. He also picked up hundreds of winner's crowns at other festivals.

LIFE IN ANCIENT GREECE

WRESTLERS

There were no weight categories in ancient Greek wrestling, so champions were usually the largest athletes with the biggest muscles. Stories tell how they were great meat eaters. The **legend** of Milon of Croton, for instance, tells how he ate a whole cow at one sitting!

Like other athletes, wrestlers oiled their bodies, but before they fought they dusted themselves with powder so they were not too slippery to grip. Fights were extremely vicious. The opening tactic of one wrestler from the ancient Greek city Sikyon was to attempt to break his opponent's fingers!

The **hoplitodromos,** a race in armor, was the final contest of the games. Athletes wearing helmets and heavy leg armor called greaves would run two lengths of the stadium carrying a large shield. It must have been exhausting to run bearing this extra weight in the heat of summer, but to the Greeks it would have been a reminder of the importance of sports as a preparation for war.

This Greek vase dates from the 400s B.C.E. and shows athletes competing in the hoplitodromos.

DAY FOUR PROGRAM OF EVENTS

MORNING
- *Wrestling*

MIDDAY
- *Boxing*
- *The pancratium—a combination of wrestling and boxing*

AFTERNOON
- *The hoplitodromos—a race in armor*

Victory at the Olympic Games was the high point of a Greek athlete's career, and the final day of the games was a day of prize-giving and celebration. The ceremonies took place outside the Temple of Zeus. The **hellanodikai** crowned each victorious athlete with a wreath woven from a leafy branch of the sacred olive tree in the **Altis.** When all the winners had been crowned, they were showered in leaves and flower petals thrown by the crowds of cheering **spectators.**

This Greek gold wreath was made in the 300s B.C.E. All winning athletes wore wreaths of leaves presented at the end of the Olympic Games.

DAY FIVE PROGRAM OF EVENTS

MORNING

- Grand **procession** of winners to the Temple of Zeus

- Presentation of victory wreaths by the hellanodikai

AFTERNOON & EVENING

- Celebrations—private parties and a banquet for winners

- Procession of winners around the Altis, singing victory hymns

This illustration on a Greek vase made in the 400s B.C.E. shows victory ribbons being awarded to athletes.

The celebration feasts that followed the games often lasted well into the night. A huge banquet was held for the winners and others, but there were private parties, too, with wine, food, speeches, and songs. For the Olympic winners, the celebrations did not end with the games. When they reached home, they were treated as heroes. There were more feasts and parties. Cash rewards and honors were also presented to them by their home city. Sometimes, a statue of the Olympic champion was made so that his fame would live on.

This bronze statue was made in Greece around 500 B.C.E. It shows an Olympic winner enjoying a celebration feast.

LIFE IN ANCIENT GREECE
COOKS

The Olympic Games were a very busy time for cooks because they had to prepare huge celebration feasts. A feast was a chance for a host to offer guests the finest wines and food and for cooks to show off their skills by serving their tastiest dishes. A typical menu might have included honey-glazed shrimp and tuna steak, followed by a whole roasted pig. Dessert would be a choice of fresh fruit and a selection of delicate pastries and cakes.

AMAZING FACT

Only Olympic winners were crowned with olive wreaths. At the Pythian games, wreaths were woven from laurel. Fresh celery or pine were used at the Isthmian games, and dried celery was used at the Nemean games.

The Fall and Rise of the Olympic Games

THE OLYMPICS THEN & NOW

ANCIENT GAMES

- *Held every four years in late summer at Olympia, in Greece*
- *Only Greek boys and men were allowed to compete*
- *Athletes competed unclothed and no second or third prizes were given*
- *The winner's reward was to be crowned with a wreath of olive leaves*
- *By 100 C.E., about 40,000 spectators were attending the Olympic Games*

MODERN GAMES

- *Since 1924, there have been separate Olympics for winter and summer sports*
- *Summer and winter games are each held every four years in a different country*
- *Men and women of all nationalities now take part*
- *Athletes wear a range of specially designed clothing*
- *Gold, silver, and bronze medals are awarded for first, second, and third place*
- *Today, a single Olympic stadium can hold about 100,000 spectators, while millions more can watch events on television*

This photograph of the closing ceremony at the 2000 Sydney Olympics shows that the Olympics were coming to Athens, Greece, in 2004.

Although Greece became part of the Roman empire in 146 B.C.E., the Olympic Games continued. The Olympics, however, gradually became more about pleasing the **spectators** than about pleasing the gods. The games were finally brought to an end by the rise of Christianity. The final ancient Olympic festival was held in about 393 C.E., when the emperor of Rome, Theodosius I, banned the worship of non-Christian gods. The Olympics had lasted more than 1,100 years.

This photograph was taken at the stadium in Athens, Greece, in 1896. It was the scene of the first modern Olympics.

In the late 1800s, Baron Pierre de Coubertin of France had the idea to bring back the Olympic Games. **Archaeologists** had begun to uncover the site of the ancient games at Olympia, and Coubertin had read about their discoveries. He also believed that international sports competitions could build friendships among nations. Coubertin's energy and enthusiasm led to the first modern Olympics in Athens in 1896. That year, a total of 311 athletes from 13 nations competed in the games.

LIFE IN ANCIENT GREECE
ARCHAEOLOGISTS

Over the centuries Olympia was destroyed by invading armies, earthquakes, and floods. Today, we owe our knowledge about the site of the ancient Olympic Games to archaeologists. The fallen buildings were gradually buried beneath rubble and river mud, and the site was forgotten.

An English archaeologist named Richard Chandler rediscovered Olympia in 1766. Archaeologists began studying the site in detail in the 1800s. The remains of temples and other buildings as well as thousands of objects have been uncovered. This helped archaeologists piece together a picture of Olympia and the ancient games.

OLYMPIC HEROES

One of the new events at the 1896 Olympic Games was the marathon, a long-distance race of about 26 miles (42 kilometers). It was won by a Greek farmer named Spiridon Louis.

This photo shows the first meeting of the International Olympic Committee, with representatives from France, Germany, Greece, Hungary, Russia, Sweden, and Bohemia (modern-day Czech Republic). Baron Pierre de Coubertin, second from left, formed the committee on June 23, 1894. Its responsibility is to look over the organization of the modern Olympic Games.

Time Line

776 B.C.E. Earliest recorded date of the Olympic Games at Olympia. From this point they are held every four years. At the first thirteen Olympic Games, there is only one event—the **stade.**

680 B.C.E. Chariot races first held

540 B.C.E. The Olympic champion Milon of Croton wins the boy's wrestling contest. In following years, he wins the men's wrestling event at five Olympic Games.

400s B.C.E. The champion boxer Theagenes of Thasos wins numerous events at the Olympic Games and other festivals during his 22-year career.

350s B.C.E. A magnificent stadium is built, the first outside the Altis.

200s B.C.E. The **palaestra** is built.

100s B.C.E. The gymnasium is built.

164–152 B.C.E. The great Olympic champion Leonidas of Rhodes wins all three running races at four Olympic Games in a row.

146 B.C.E. All the Greek city-states become part of the Roman empire.

80 B.C.E. The Roman general Sulla orders the Olympic Games to be held in Rome. They return to Olympia after his death two years later.

390s C.E. The final ancient Olympic Games are held, around the time that the worship of non-Christian gods is banned by the emperor of Rome, Theodosius I.

400s C.E. The site at Olympia suffers the beginnings of centuries of damage. Destroyed by invading armies, earthquakes, and flooding, it is gradually forgotten.

426 C.E. The Temple of Zeus is destroyed by fire.

1766 Olympia is rediscovered by the English **archaeologist** Richard Chandler.

1875 German archaeologists begin major excavations at Olympia.

1896 The first modern Olympic Games are held in Athens. There are 42 events, with 311 contestants from 13 countries. The first-ever marathon is won by Spiridon Louis of Greece.

1900 Women are first allowed to compete in the Olympic Games, in the tennis event.

1996 One hundred years after the first modern Olympics, the Olympics are held in Atlanta, Georgia. There are 271 events, with 10,768 contestants from 79 countries.

2004 The Olympic Games are held in Athens, Greece.

More Books to Read

Middleton, Haydn. *Ancient Greek Jobs.* Chicago: Heinemann Library, 2002.

Middleton, Haydn. *Ancient Greek War and Weapons.* Chicago: Heinemann Library, 2002.

Middleton, Haydn. *Ancient Olympic Games.* Chicago: Heinemann Library, 1999.

Ross, Stewart. *The Original Olympics.* Columbus, Ohio: McGraw-Hill Children's Publishing, 1999.

Tames, Richard. *Ancient Greek Children.* Chicago: Heinemann Library, 2002.

Woff, Richard. *The Ancient Greek Olympics.* New York: Oxford University Press, 2000.

Glossary

altar raised structure or place on which sacrifices are offered in worship. An altar can also be a table or platform used as a center of worship.

Altis sacred space in Olympia that was enclosed by walls

archaeologist person who studies past human life and activities by looking closely at fossils, tools, monuments, and other remains

citizen person who lives in a city or town

city-state city and its surrounding territory, which is governed by the people living there

colonnade row of building columns that often support a roof

colony group of people living in a new place but who are still ruled by people in the place they moved from. People who live in a colony are called colonists.

democracy system in which the government is elected by the people. A thing or place that uses this type of system is called democratic.

diaulos running race of about 1,310 feet (400 meters)

dolichos race of about 4,600 to 5,900 feet (1,400 to 1,800 meters)

fertility condition of being able to develop and grow

hellanodikes judge of the ancient Olympic Games. More than one are called *hellanodikai*.

herald person who announces important news

hippodrome arena in which horse-related sporting events took place in ancient Greece

hoplitodromos race in which competitors wore full armor

laurel type of evergreen tree. Its leaves were used to make a wreath to crown a winner of the Pythian games.

legend popular story handed down from earlier times that is not necessarily true but that many people believe

palaestra ancient Olympic wrestling school

pancratium event involving a combination of wrestling and boxing

philosopher person who studies and thinks in order to become wiser

poleis city-states of ancient Greece

procession group of people moving along in an orderly, ceremonial way, as if they were in a parade

ritual act that is repeated over and over again. It could be religious or for a ceremony.

sacrifice symbolic killing or offering of something to please a god or goddess

sanctuary holy or safe place or a hideaway

slave person owned by another person or a person forced to do what another person tells him or her to do

spectator person who watches an event, such as a soccer game

stade running race of about 630 feet (192 meters)

Index